COME BACK TO ME
WITH ALL YOUR HEART

REFLECTIONS ON LENT

Tony Flannery

First published 2004 by
Veritas Publications
7/8 Lower Abbey Street
Dublin 1
Ireland
Email publications@veritas.ie
Website www.veritas.ie

ISBN 1 85390 797 9

10 9 8 7 6 5 4 3 2 1

A catalogue record for this book is available from the British Library.

Printed in the Republic of Ireland by Betaprint Ltd

Veritas books are printed on paper made from the wood pulp of managed forests. For
every tree felled, at least one tree is planted, thereby renewing natural resources.

Contents

1

Lent

The word 'Lent' has gone into general use. To describe something as lenten means that it is spartan and difficult. The traditional image of the Lenten observance, as we knew it in the Catholic Church up to recent times, was undoubtedly spartan. Lent was about doing penance, and, in particular, fasting. Like Jesus in the desert, we had to fast for forty days. And it was a fairly strict fast, with just one full meal, and two of what were called collations. These were hard enough to define, because their content varied from place to place. But at their best they were light meals. Friday had the added dimension of having to abstain from meat. In my boarding school days the authorities were no believers in the nourishment of fish, so for the Fridays of Lent our dinner consisted of two fried eggs, with some vegetable and potato, but no attempt at any type of sauce or gravy. Even by the standards of the time it was a poor dinner, lacking in sustenance and flavour. Like almost everything else in the Church at the time, the Lenten fast was imposed under pain of serious sin. Unless you were young, old or in bad health, and could get a derivation from your local priest, you had to fast or risk the pains of Hell.

Lent was also a sombre time. All the statues and pictures in the church were covered with purple cloth. Flowers were banished, and an alleluia or a Gloria would not be heard again until Easter. All of this had a certain charm about it, and it is easy to look back with a degree of nostalgia. But it is worth looking at the underlying message that was coming through. Undoubtedly, the love of God for humanity was part of that message, in that he was willing to suffer and die for our salvation. But there was an overriding emphasis on our sin, particularly personal sins. We were led to believe that we were miserable creatures, steeped in evil and sin. While there is some truth in this, the emphasis given to it easily led to the belief that salvation was scarce and hard to achieve, and that most would fail, and be lost. This led to the damaging assumption that the forgiveness and mercy of God were somewhat miserly. He was a hard taskmaster, and would only be generous to a few. This type of message generated the fear that many of us remember from our early years, but another result of it was possibly even more destructive. Many people became cautious and careful in their lives. There was too much at stake, and salvation was earned most of all by avoiding sin. Keep out of any situation that might lead us into sin, the remote or proximate occasions, as they were called, and we would be all right. The statement of Jesus that he had come that we might have the fullness of life didn't get much of an airing!

Since I have had a chance to study the Bible I can see that the Scriptural idea of Lent, and of salvation generally, was much more positive, with the emphasis more on life than on death, on salvation than damnation.

One of the great Scriptural sentences that touch at the heart of Lent is from the Prophet Joel, and we hear it in the first reading of Ash Wednesday:

Come back to me with all your heart.

What is being referred to here is the direction our life is taking, and the values and attitudes by which we live. But most of all it is about living. There is so much in the Lenten Scripture readings about life, and about living it with courage and enthusiasm. That was the part of Lent that we missed. Our religion, because of the excessive emphasis on personal sin, and the apparent difficulty of salvation, had become for many a hindrance to living rather than an encouragement. I suspect that is partly why some of the great minds of Ireland in the last century, artists and writers, turned away from the faith. They could see that the version of the Christian message that was being presented was an obstacle in the way of people living their lives.

This book is a small effort at trying to rediscover this more positive Lenten message. That does not mean that we give up on penance and fasting. They too are integral parts of living life to the full. Our human nature is flawed. There is a weakness in us that can lead us into slavery, slavery to our own desires and addictions. The heart of every human being has an inclination towards evil that must be curtailed. Any cursory examination of the world in which we live will attest to that. The old doctrine of original sin is an attempt to explain where this evil came from. But whatever its origins, it is a part of ourselves that we must recognise.

The Gospel reading for the first Sunday of Lent is the story of the temptations of Jesus. We are told he spent forty days in the desert, fasting and praying, and during that time he was tempted by the devil. I am sure we are into figurative language here, and it is hard to know what exactly was the reality of Jesus' experience during that time. But the temptations he endured were very human ones, that we are all familiar with, temptations to use his talents and abilities in order to become wealthy, famous and have power over people.

If you are the Son of God tell these stones to turn into loaves.
I will give you all these, if you fall at my feet and worship me.

He battled with these tendencies and came out triumphant, through the help of bodily penance and prayer.

Be off Satan! For Scripture says: You must worship the Lord your God and serve him alone.

We need to do the same. But we do it not in order to win salvation from a miserly God. It is to gain our freedom, freedom from the weakness and evil within us, the tendencies that would enslave us.

We are gone from the days when the Church laid down in detail how we should do penance. That is only as it should be. The emphasis now is on taking responsibility for our own lives. Not to do penance of any nature just because it is no longer a strict law of the Church would not be a healthy or mature response on our part. In whatever way you choose, it is good to do battle with yourself, to learn to say 'no' to yourself, and in that way to gain freedom.

Without being in any way an expert on the raising of children, it does seem to me that there is a great danger today that parents will spoil their children by giving them everything they want. We are experiencing the first generation in this country when many parents are in a position to meet all the material needs and demands of their children. If they succumb to this, then the child will never learn the vital importance of self-discipline. Without self-discipline life can veer out of control, and end up in misery.

The fundamental idea of Lent then, as I understand it, is to learn to control or discipline ourselves so that we can live that fullness of life that Jesus came to bring us. During these six weeks, in whatever way we can, we try to live our lives in a new way, and to repent of our past failures and inadequacies.

The classic statement of repentance is Psalm 50. It is worth spending time over.

Have mercy on me, God, in your kindness.
In your compassion wash out my offence.
O wash me more and more from my guilt
and cleanse me from my sin.

My offences truly I know them;
my sin is always before me.
Against you, you alone, have I sinned:
what is evil in your sight I have done.

A pure heart create for me, O God,
put a steadfast spirit within me.
Do not cast me away from your presence,
nor deprive me of your holy spirit.

Give me again the joy of your help;
with a spirit of fervour sustain me.
O Lord, open my lips
and my mouth shall declare your praise.

2

The Word of God is Alive and Active

Lent is a time, maybe more than any other time, for contemplating the Word of God.

The variety and richness of the Word presented to us during the Masses of Lent, especially the Sundays and Holy Week readings, gives great scope for contemplation.

I trust those two sentences, as an introduction, are not enough to put the average reader off. Contemplating the Word of God is not something most Irish Catholics are used to, certainly not in any structured sense. It is read at Mass, sometimes well read and sometimes badly, and largely passes over our heads, or at best makes only a slight impact that is quickly forgotten. Many of the readings are much too difficult to be grasped with just one reading. The idea of taking the readings home in the Sunday leaflet to study them, or looking them up in our Bible, is not something that most people would even consider.

And yet the Word of God is important to a Christian. The Bible, though it is quite a difficult book, gives us unparalleled access to the life and thoughts of God. The Letter to the Hebrews puts it well:

The Word of God is something alive and active; it cuts more incisively than any two-edged sword; it can seek out the place where soul is divided from spirit, or joints from marrow; it can pass judgement on secret emotions and thoughts. No created thing is hidden from him; everything is uncovered and stretched full open to the eyes of the one to whom we must give account of ourselves.

God is ever present in our lives, no matter what the state of our belief. He is present with us in love, because he made us and calls us by our name. We cannot hide from God. He knows us through and through.

O Lord, you search me and you know me,
you know my resting and my rising,
you discern my purpose from afar,
you mark when I walk or lie down.
All my ways lie open to you.

In the story of Jesus' temptations during his forty-day fast in the desert, an important Lenten story which I will deal with more fully later, he tells us that his word is essential for life.

Human beings live not on bread alone, but on every word that comes from the mouth of God.

And he goes on to make a great promise. His word repays the effort and time needed to hear it properly, indeed it repays us a hundredfold.

If you make my word your home, you will indeed be my disciples; you will learn the truth and the truth will set you free.

The Word of God will set us free, because it is a Word of Love, a Word of Life.

The old Penny Catechism, as it was known, quoted Ignatius of Loyola telling us that God made us to 'know, love and serve him in this world, and to be happy with him forever in Heaven'.

According to Desmond O'Donnell OMI this image of God, an image of benevolence and dominance, is no longer credible.

> *Only the God of Jesus, who made us to 'have life and have it to the full', only the God who, according to the New Catechism, 'freely created us to share his own blessed life and at every time and in every place draws close to us', only the God whom we are privileged to call 'Abba', only that God can call us to the total surrender of faith.*

This book is an effort to present some of these readings, and the ideas contained in them, in an easy, accessible way. I will take the big themes of Lent, and try to give food for reflection and prayer on them. But most of all I will focus on some of the great Gospel stories, particularly the ones found in the Gospel of John, and attempt to bring them to life by presenting them in a fresh way.

Most of all, this little book is a small effort at helping us to come to know God, through reflection on his Word.

3

The Strange Story of Abraham and Isaac

Before we go any farther in contemplating the Word of God, it is good to put in a note of caution. Religions of all shades and beliefs have been a source of war and conflict at various times down through the ages. The same is still happening today. For example, the behaviour of certain factions of fundamentalist Muslim belief are frightening. People seem to believe that God is telling them to kill and destroy other human beings, and that they will be rewarded in the next life for doing so. Christianity fought many religious wars with something of the same type of mentality at work. When religious belief narrows, and when people are convinced that their belief is right and that everyone else is wrong, the potential for conflict and destruction is great.

We have to conclude that religion is not always a totally positive blessing. It needs to be understood and interpreted properly, or it can go badly awry.

The Christian book on which our faith is based, the Bible, is a difficult book, not easily understood. Some Christian denominations teach that every sentence in the Bible can be interpreted literally as the Word of God. When this is pushed to the extreme it can be dangerous.

Let us take the story of Abraham and Isaac as an example of a story that needs to be interpreted properly.

The readings for the second Sunday in Lent contain this strange story, in which God puts Abraham to the test by asking him to sacrifice his only son, Isaac.

> *Take your son, your only child Isaac, whom you love, and go to the land of Moriah. There you shall offer him as a burnt offering, on a mountain I will point out to you.*

Abraham did as he was told, and when he had the knife raised, ready to kill his poor little Isaac, the voice of an angel spoke.

> *Do not raise your hand against the boy. Do not harm him, for now I know you fear God. You have not refused me your son, your only son.*

Moses then sacrificed a ram instead. We are not told what effect this incident had on the young boy. In today's world he would be going to a tribunal looking for compensation for the emotional damage done to him! My assumption is that this is an apocryphal story, told to make a point rather than to be taken at a literal level. It is hard to believe that God, as we have come to know him, would ask something of this nature of any father, even as a test. I know it is also seen as a prophetic reference to the coming of Jesus, and how God allowed his own Son to be sacrificed for our salvation.

The book of Genesis goes on to tell us that, after Abraham had given this proof of his faith, God made him a promise. It comes in two versions, differently expressed, but both saying basically the same thing.

> *I will shower blessings on you, I will make your descendants as many as the stars of heaven and the grains of sand on the seashore. Your descendants shall gain possession of the gates of their enemies.*

More specifically and dramatically, God promises in another part of Genesis:

> *To your descendants I give this land,*
> *From the wadi of Egypt to the Great River.*

It would be hard to find any other sentence in the Bible, or indeed in other literature, that has caused so much war, destruction and death as these sentences, right down to our own time and the interminable conflict going on in the Middle East. Clearly some of the sentiments expressed in the promise are contrary to the basic message of our faith. Taking possession of the gates of our enemies is a far cry from the command to forgive our enemies, and grabbing land where other people have lived for centuries and driving them out is hardly very Christian behaviour either.

So we must be careful in our use of the Bible, and avoid any type of fundamentalist or literal interpretation. Jesus, in his preaching of the Kingdom of God, wants us to open our eyes and ears, to be willing to see things in a new way, rather than closing in on ourselves with self-righteous beliefs and attitudes.

When dealing with the Bible, particularly the Old Testament, it is better to read it with a figurative rather than a literal frame of mind, looking for the meaning behind the statements and stories rather than what they seem to say on the surface. And whatever you read, measure it against the overall message of the book, especially the message of Jesus in the New Testament.

4

The Symbolism of Ashes

Why is it that there are often more people in Church on Ash Wednesday to get ashes put on their forehead than there are at Sunday Mass?

In the Old Testament ashes were used as a sign of repentance. When the prophets called on the people to repent, the rulers would dress themselves in sackcloth and sprinkle themselves with ashes. It was a sign that they were determined to change their lives, to turn away from sin and evil.

Change of life is a central Lenten idea, but I think the appeal of the ashes to the ordinary believer is something different. The Ash Wednesday ritual touches people at a deep level. It goes to the heart of the most basic fears and anxieties of the human being. The traditional formula that was used as the ashes were placed on our foreheads states it in a bald and direct fashion:

Remember man, thou art but dust, and unto dust thou shalt return.

Its modern alternative, while containing its own important message, is not quite so stark.

Turn away from sin and believe the Gospel.

But, old or modern, ashes have an appeal because the reality of decay and death is inescapable. It creeps up on all of us, and sometimes comes suddenly or violently. The shadow of death is a constant companion throughout life. It can be the great enemy, the ultimate defeat that we do all in our power to postpone for as long as possible. That is very much the way the modern world looks on it. Keeping healthy and fit has become the new morality. The ultimate sin is to be living an unhealthy lifestyle, and the ultimate waste is to die young.

Attempting to escape from the reality of decay and death is an absorbing activity for many, as they lose themselves in work, sport, or some other aspect of life. Of course the attempt is ultimately futile, because hiding from it won't change the inevitability of death, and we can easily become addicted to which ever form of escape we choose.

The Christian message that comes through the Lenten period has plenty to say about death, and is full of the promise of eternal life. I will just take a few examples, maybe some that are not the obvious ones we hear so often.

The story of Moses and the burning bush is interesting and colourful, and like all Bible stories it can be read at many levels. The Jews were in slavery in Egypt, and they endured a miserable existence, constantly pining for their own land. When Moses saw the bush burning, but not being consumed, he was curious and he approached to see what was happening. God spoke from the bush,

> *Take off your shoes, because the ground on which you walk is holy ground.*

This established the nature of the voice from the bush; it was not just any voice, it was the voice of the Lord.

I have seen the miserable state of my people in Egypt. I have heard their appeal to be free of their slave drivers. Yes, I am aware of their sufferings. I mean to deliver them out of the hands of the Egyptians and bring them up out of that land to a land rich and broad, a land where milk and honey flow.

This promise of God to his people in slavery in Egypt is also a promise to us. We are not trapped in this world of decay and death. There is a means of escape, and there is another land, another life. I know it is figurative language, not to be interpreted literally, but the phrase 'a land rich and broad, a land where milk and honey flow' is beautiful, and full of an expectation which I like to believe refers to eternity.

St Paul has a different way of putting it, somewhat less colourful as is his wont, but the idea is the same:

Though your body may be dead it is because of sin, if Christ is in you then your spirit is life itself... and if the Spirit of him who raised Jesus from the dead is living in you, then he who raised Jesus from the dead will give life to your own mortal bodies through his Spirit living in you.

But this promise, this hope, did not come easy. Jesus had to earn our freedom through tasting the harsh reality of life, the reality that is symbolised by the ashes, in his own body. Isaiah, in the Good Friday reading, prophesies what awaits him:

Without beauty, without majesty we saw him,
No looks to attract our eyes;
a thing despised and rejected by men,

a man of sorrows and familiar with suffering,
a man to make people screen their faces;
he was despised and we took no account of him.
And yet ours were the sufferings he bore,
ours the sorrows he carried...
like a lamb he was led to the slaughter
like a sheep that is dumb before its shearers
never opening his mouth.

Suffering and death continue to be part of the human experience. They still remain the most baffling questions about the meaning of life and of our personal existence, but now we can look beyond them. Some of the awfulness has been taken away. Jesus has cast a new light on this dark side of life, and made it more endurable.

His soul's anguish over
he shall see the light and be content.

We trust that for us too the soul's anguish will come to an end. We have to struggle through the painful experience of decay and death in this world, but we believe that we shall also see the light and be content. That promise has made all the difference.

5

The Kingdom of God

The time is here;
The Kingdom of God is at hand;
Repent, and believe the Good News. (Mark, Ch. 1)

Scholars now suggest that this may have been the first public statement of Jesus. It is short and pithy, but it contains his core message. For the next three years he would try by every means in his power to elaborate and explain this message, mostly using images and speaking in parables.

Did you ever wonder if Jesus knew that he was the Son of God from the first moment of his existence here on earth? Did he open his eyes in that stable in Bethlehem and say to himself: 'Here I am. I am the Son of God and I have come to save the world'. Of course we can't be sure of the answer to that question. It touches on the area of the relationship between the humanity and the divinity of Jesus. And in this we are into the world of mystery, a world our minds cannot understand. To say that Jesus was both God and man is at one level an impossibility, a contradiction in terms. To be God would, by definition, preclude being also human, and vice versa. So we can make no definite statements about how this mystery worked itself out in the everyday life of Jesus. We have no access to his inner life.

But many scholars today believe that he was not aware of his real identity and mission until he reached maturity. It seems to make sense to suggest that Jesus came to an awareness of himself in the same way that we ourselves do. It is obvious from reading about his words and actions that he was a person of great clarity of thought and sharp judgement, with a particular ability to assess people and situations. We already have an example of him at the age of twelve asking questions of the teachers in the temple, and clearly they were questions well beyond the understanding of the normal twelve-year-old. So we know he was someone who asked the basic questions about himself and life. And presumably through study, reflection and prayer he gradually came to the answers. He learned who he was and what his mission and purpose in life was to be. Then, sometime in his late twenties, he felt ready to begin. All Mark's gospel tells us is that he went to Gallilee, his home place, and began to proclaim the Good News.

> *The time is here;*
> *The Kingdom of God is at hand.*
> *Repent, and believe the Good News.*

We have no information on Jesus' style of delivery, whither he proclaimed in a loud clear voice, or if he spoke quietly, depending on the power of what he had to say to make an impression on people. Of course he had no microphones, so he must have been capable of speaking strongly when he addressed crowds of thousands of people. Neither do we know what the people who heard him made of this first public proclamation of

Jesus. Did people think he was gone mad, or suffering from his nerves? He seems to have lived a quiet life up to this point, probably working in the same business as Joseph. Though it is hard to believe that he wasn't already showing some signs of what was to come in the future. One thing is certain, from the moment Jesus gave this talk, things would never be the same again.

All through his public life Jesus tended to speak in images, and the 'Kingdom of God' (sometimes translated as the 'Kingdom of Heaven') is one of the most common images he used, and one that has often been misinterpreted. The presumption has been that when Jesus used this image he was talking about Heaven, or salvation. There is a story of him meeting a rich young man, who was living a blameless life. Jesus put a further challenge to him:

> *Go, and sell all you have and give the money to the poor, and you will have riches in Heaven. Then come, and follow me.*

We are told the man went away sad, because he was so wealthy. Jesus' comment was that it is harder for a camel to pass through the eye of a needle than for a rich person to enter the Kingdom of God. This sentence has caused lots of problems down through the ages. Even the apostles assumed that he was talking about salvation.

> *But who then can be saved?*

It is probable that what Jesus had in mind had more to do with this life than the next. When he talked about the Kingdom of God he was proposing a new way of looking at things, a radically new attitude to life that would involve a new way of living. There are three core values or planks to this vision. They are powerful in their simplicity.

- Instead of all the enmity, division and hatred, if people could learn to love each other, then the world would be a much happier place for all.
- Instead of being at war with their neighbours, if people could learn to be at peace, there would be an end to all the misery and suffering that war brings.
- The resources of the world are sufficient to meet everyone's needs. If only people were not so greedy, and shared what they had with each other, then every human being would have a decent chance in life.

The last sentence of Jesus' short talk, *'Repent and believe the Good News'*, sums it all up. The original of that word, 'repent' carried a broader and stronger meaning than the word does for us today. The original meaning had more to do with taking a new look at things, beginning to see things with new eyes. This new way of looking is essential if we are to recognise the vision of Jesus. It isn't easy. All of us, due to our upbringing, our education, the various prejudices and attitudes we learn along the way, develop certain ways of looking at ourselves, others and life. And it is tempting to hold on to those views, because we have become comfortable with them. New ways of looking at things are challenging, because they will inevitably ask us to change to new attitudes and actions.

So when Jesus talked about how hard it was for the rich man to enter the Kingdom of God he was talking about what effect the pursuit of material things has on a person. It narrows his outlook. He can no longer see things clearly or broadly. With his focus on material gain he inevitably becomes greedy and selfish, and he can no longer see other people for what they are, but rather how they can be of use to himself. That is why Jesus wanted the young man to give all his wealth away; it was corrupting him, blinding him, preventing him from seeing in a new or different way. Jesus wanted to set him free. So it was in that sense that Jesus meant a rich person would find it hard to enter the Kingdom of God. He was making a statement of fact, not an eternal judgement.

Equally, in that passage from Luke's Gospel where the apostles are recounting tragedies from the past and asking Jesus to explain them, if they were the result of sin, he responds with the sentence;

> *Unless you repent, you will all perish as they did.*

If they continue to look on life in the old way, the way of hatred, division and violence, then many more will undoubtedly suffer and die. That is the inevitable consequence of the old way of looking at things. But with a new vision, with new eyes to see, things would really begin to change.

For three years Jesus preached this message, constantly using images to try to communicate the Kingdom of God.

> *The Kingdom of God is …*

At the end of that time they killed him. And of course the religious leaders were to the fore in trying to get rid of him. They had learned to hate him so much because his teaching was upsetting everything, it was turning the values of society and church upside down. And the simplicity of it all made it extraordinarily effective.

But though they managed to kill his body, they did not stifle the message. Two thousand years later there are still many of us who are inspired by this man, whom we believe was God, and by his vision. We still gather to hear his word, and to celebrate our faith in him. We know that he did not stay dead, but that he rose from the tomb, and is alive and present with us. We know too that we are a long way from bringing the Kingdom of God into practice, but we can see the wisdom of it, and that it is worth aiming for.

St Paul puts it this way:

> *With Christ there is a new creation; the old creation is gone, and a new one is here.*

In Lent we try to hasten this new creation, in our own lives and in the world around us.

6

The Water of Life (Jn, Ch. 4)

Christianity makes considerable use of symbols. When we are trying to understand God and the things of the spirit, we are in a realm that is outside the grasp of our minds, so symbols can help to lead us into the mystery. Water is one of the great Christian symbols. In the early Old Testament water is destructive in the story of the great flood, destroying all living things except those who entered the Ark with Noah. When the flood had receded, God made a covenant, an agreement with his people.

> *No thing of flesh shall be swept away again by the flood. There shall be no flood to destroy the earth again.*

From then on water became a positive symbol, a symbol of life.

> *Tormented by thirst the people complained against Moses.*

The people in question were the Jews during their forty years crossing the desert after their escape from slavery in Egypt. No doubt about it, but water, essential to life in general, is especially so in the desert, and the people were clearly getting desperate. Moses turned to God:

A little more and they will stone me.

He clearly wasn't very secure in his leadership role. Under God's direction he strikes the rock at Horeb, and water gushes out. The image is powerful. A large gathering of thirsty people gulping down the clear fresh water out of the rock. It was an image that obviously impressed Jesus, because he often referred to water as an illustration of the new life he had come to bring.

Of all the stories about Jesus in the Gospels, my favourite is the one about his meeting with a woman at a well in Samaria in the middle of a hot day. I think it is a story that gives us a rounded picture of the sort of person Jesus was, and what he stood for – the real Jesus.

> *Jesus came to a Samaritan town called Sychar. Jacob's well was there and Jesus, tired by the journey, sat down by the well. It was about noon. A Samaritan woman came to draw some water.*

There were many reasons why Jesus should not have spoken to the woman who came to that well in Samaria, when he had stopped for a rest and some refreshment to help cope with the heat of the day. He would not have expected her to be there in the first place. Running water in homes was a luxury confined to only the most noble of Roman families at the time, so all the rest had to go to the well for water for drinking, cooking and hygiene. It was the woman's job to fetch and carry that water. But they invariably went to the well in the early morning, before the heat of the day built up. It would be most unusual, because of the heat, for someone to come at noon, which was the time Jesus was there. So the fact that the woman came at this time may have indicated that she was avoiding the other women, or was not accepted by them. She may have been something of an outcast. As the story unfolds we learn a possible explanation for that. But first some cultural background.

Jews did not fraternise with Samaritans. The Samaritans had let the side down some hundreds of years previously by intermarrying with a pagan tribe, and taking on some of their customs and religious practices. For instance, they no longer went to Jerusalem once a year to pray and offer sacrifice, as all good Jews were supposed to do. Instead they went to a mountain in Samaria. Those Jews who regarded themselves as orthodox reacted by ostracising the Samaritans.

There was another reason why Jesus should not have spoken to this woman. By this time he had become recognised as a rabbi, a man of learning and holiness. The Jews were great lawmakers, and there were many laws governing the life and behaviour of rabbis. They were particularly forbidden from engaging in conversation with a woman on her own. It would be a cause of scandal, as can be seen by the surprise of the disciples when they returned from the village and found him talking to her.

So, when Jesus asked the woman for a drink of water she was amazed.

> You are a Jew, and I am a Samaritan, so how can you ask me for a drink?

Jesus immediately takes the conversation to a whole new level, and there is no indication that the woman had any idea of what he was talking about.

> If only you knew what God gives, and who it is that is asking you for a drink, you would ask him, and he would give you life-giving water.

This is typical of the way Jesus is presented in John's Gospel. He is constantly offering life, the bread of life, the water of life, I have come that you may have life. Clearly the writer of John's gospel saw Jesus most of all as a life-giver. But the woman is sceptical, and practical, so she asks him how can he get this water without a bucket. His answer is even more baffling.

> *The water that I will give you will become a spring inside you, giving you life-giving water, and leading to eternal life.*

One thing you would have to say about Jesus is that he was never miserly in the promises he made to people! But the woman is still thinking on a practical level.

> *Give me that water. Then I will never be thirsty again, and will not have to come here to draw water.*

That would take some of the pressure from her life.

But in order for this new life that Jesus brings to flourish in us, we need to free ourselves from all the obstacles that we create in our daily living. So Jesus changes the conversation, and confronts her in the area where she is experiencing greatest weakness.

> *Go and call your husband, and come back.*

From the way the story is written you can feel the tension in the air, the woman going silent and turning away, and then slowly, with all the pain and weariness of a life that has gone all wrong, she answers:

I haven't got a husband.

How Jesus knew about her marital history we don't know, but he was a shrewd observer of people and he could probably read a lot from the expression on her face. He compliments her for her honesty. The woman is clearly impressed.

I see you are a prophet, sir.

But she tries to evade the issue by changing the subject, bringing up the big point of contention between Jews and Samaritans. Is it necessary for all Jews to worship God at the temple in Jerusalem? Jesus again takes the conversation to a new level in his response.

Believe me, the hour is coming when you will worship the Father neither on this mountain nor in Jerusalem… a time when true worshippers will worship the Father in spirit and in truth.

This seems to make sense to the woman, and she is beginning to understand the level at which Jesus is talking. She is no longer concerned about the water in the well. She too has gone back to basics, the promise, the hope of a Messiah, a saviour.

I know that the Messiah is coming, and when he comes he will tell us everything.

The answer Jesus gave her certainly got through to her.

I am he. I who am talking to you, I am the Messiah.

Now there was no confusion, because as the disciples came back she raced into the village. She was clearly a new person, full of enthusiasm, and the people could see the change in her.

> *Come, come and see the man who has told me everything I ever did.* [A slight bit of exaggeration is understandable in the circumstances!] *Could he be the Messiah?*

This made them so curious that they stopped what they were doing and went out to the well to see Jesus.

The scholars suggest that this was the first time that Jesus told anyone of his real identity. If the theory is correct that he only gradually came to a realisation of his own identity, it is possible that his encounter with this woman was the event that finally convinced him of who he was. Telling her was typical of the sort of thing that Jesus did. She was the least likely person that he might have told, just as the shepherds were the least likely people to be given the 'tidings of great joy' at Christmastime. Why didn't he attempt to go to the High Priest, or the Governor, people who might be able to help him in his mission? Instead he told a Samaritan woman with five husbands! It seems to me he did it because he realised that this woman needed hope, she needed something and someone to believe in. And she became his first apostle, the first person to go out and preach about him. 'Come and see ....'

I love the picture of Jesus that comes across in this story. He had an extraordinary empathy with people. And he was a person who was so free in himself that he was able to rise above the laws, customs and prejudices of his time when he recognised a person in need. The ancient divisions and bitterness between Jews and Samaritans didn't influence him in the slightest, because when he looked at this woman he clearly did not see a Samaritan, he saw the woman for what she was in herself. And that was all that mattered to him. What he wanted to give to her was new life, a new way of looking at herself and the world, in other words, the Kingdom of God.

But it is also clear from this story why so much opposition built up to Jesus. He was a revolutionary figure in the fullest sense of that word. He promoted a radically alternative view of life and of relating to one another. Gradually he began to be a threat to the whole social and religious order, the order that forbade contact with women, the order that said Jews were better than Samaritans, and the vested interests came to see that unless they put a stop to him, he could put them out of business. So, there was a sense of inevitability about how the story would unfold. How precisely it might happen was uncertain, but it must have been plain to see for some time that they were going to try to get rid of him. He was just too much of a threat.

The challenge for us is substantial. The Christian, the person who is trying to follow Christ, needs, like Jesus, to have an alternative voice that is different from the accepted voices in society, and live by alternative values, the values of the Kingdom. This is difficult.

The ultimate aim of a believer in Jesus is to echo the words of the people from the Samaritan village, after Jesus had acceded to their request and stayed two days with them. They listened to him, and then told the woman;

> *Now we no longer believe because of what you told us; we have heard him ourselves and we know that he really is the saviour of the world.*

7

The Blind Man is Cured (Jn, Ch. 9)

The stories in John's Gospel, in the form they have come to us, were not written down for nearly a hundred years after the ascension of Jesus. So they are not meant to be accurate historical accounts of what actually happened. The conversations that are recounted in the stories are unlikely to be the exact words that Jesus used. There was a different dynamic at work. The writer, or writers, of the Gospel were more interested in giving a picture of the Jesus they had come to know through faith, the Jesus who was the central feature of their community and personal lives. This does not make the stories untrue; rather they are true at a different and deeper level than our normal understanding of truth. They give us a more whole and fuller picture of the person he was, the way he related to people, and the message he brought to humanity.

The story of Jesus curing a blind man, and his conflict with the Pharisees over his actions, is full of this deeper level of meaning. It is told in such a way as to give us a picture of the steps a person goes through in coming to know Jesus and developing faith in him. It is not a story that gives up its meaning on a casual reading, but one which repays a bit of time and effort. It will help to illuminate our own journey of faith, and our efforts to get to know Jesus.

When Jesus and his disciples saw the blind man, the disciples asked a question which showed that they still laboured under some of the misconceptions of Old Testament teaching.

Who sinned, this man or his parents, for him to have been born blind?

Jesus quickly dismisses this idea.

Neither he nor his parents sinned. He was born blind so that the works of God might be displayed in him.

But his answer doesn't throw too much light on the overall problem of suffering. In some sense, the question remains.

There is symbolic significance in the actual way Jesus carries out the cure. Having put some clay on the man's eyes he asked him to go to the pool of Siloam, and wash. On washing his sight is restored. There is a reference here to the waters of baptism, which would have been administered mostly to adults in those times, so the people at the time the story was written would more easily recognise the reference than we would. It is telling us that in taking on the new life of Christ in Baptism, and committing ourselves to following him, we begin to see things in a whole new way. Our eyes are opened. We become inhabitants of the Kingdom of God. The journey of faith has begun.

Naturally there was considerable excitement among the man's friends and neighbours when they discovered he was cured. He had been blind all his life, and now he could see. They asked him who had done this for him. His answer is significant.

The man called Jesus.

And when they asked where was he, he replied,

I don't know.

So at this stage the man knows nothing about Jesus, except his name, and doesn't know where he has gone.

When the attention of the Pharisees is drawn to the healing they are not happy. They show their legal rigidity by complaining that Jesus had cured the man on the Sabbath. The simple act of making the paste that he put on the man's eyes was enough to violate the Sabbath, and make him into a sinner. And that raised questions as to where his power came from.

This man cannot be from God; he does not keep the Sabbath.

Because he was a sinner he could not have the power to heal. The Pharisees are making a number of the sort of basic mistakes that we often make. They are presuming they can judge a person's life by externals, who is a sinner and who isn't. And they also conclude that sinners are all bad and capable of no good at all. Their view is narrow and judgmental.

So they called the man who had been blind, and questioned him. He explained exactly what had happened, and that it was Jesus who had cured him. The Pharisees were divided in their opinions, so they asked the man what he thought of Jesus. The man had advanced in his belief at this stage.

He is a prophet.

He had come to the second stage of faith. He recognised Jesus as a great teacher.

Next the Pharisees called the man's parents and questioned them. Was this their son, had he been blind, and could he now see? They confirmed his identity, but would not get involved further, out of fear of the Pharisees.

He is old enough, ask himself.

We are being told here that real faith is a personal, adult decision.

The next encounter between the man and the Pharisees is more robust. He has clearly grown in confidence, and is well able to hold up his end. He freely admits that he now regards himself as a disciple of Jesus, and asks them,

Do you want to become his disciples too?

He must have had a sense of humour – of the absurd – or was it a genuine wish to help them to have faith in Jesus?

The Pharisees revert to the old Jewish attitude that the disciples began with, presuming on the man's sinfulness because he was blind.

Are you trying to teach us, and you a sinner through and through.

And they drove him away.

Then the story tells us that Jesus went in search of the man, and this immensely significant conversation took place.

Do you believe in the Son of Man?
Sir, tell me who he is that I may believe in him.

You are looking at him; he is speaking to you.
Lord, I believe.

So there we have the different stages of faith. When the man's eyes were opened he saw 'a man called Jesus' but did not know any more. Then later, as he came to deeper awareness and greater insight, he proclaimed Jesus as a prophet. This led to his desire to follow Jesus and finally the ultimate statement of faith: 'Lord, I believe'.

The story ends where it began, on the theme that runs right through Lent, on the idea of seeing things in a new way, opening our eyes.

I have come into this world,
so that those without sight may see
and those with sight turn blind.

The Pharisees, constantly sensitive to what Jesus was saying, and probably with good reason, asked if he was referring to them, if he considered them blind.

Blind! If you were you would not be guilty, but since you say you can
see your guilt remains.

These words challenge us today. Are we blind? The disturbing thing for us who call ourselves Christians is that it was precisely the ones who considered they knew it all, the righteous ones who were living good lives and observing the laws, that Jesus condemned as the most blind of all.

This is an immensely significant story. Christianity is not first and foremost a religion of beliefs and dogma; neither is it a collection of commandments and moral guidelines. It is belief in a person, Jesus Christ. That is the essential element of it. Everything else comes secondary. The Christian is the one who is attracted by Jesus, drawn to him, fascinated by him, and ultimately recognises him as the Lord of his life. Everything else, beliefs and commandments, follow from this, and without the personal faith in Jesus they are no more than empty formulas.

The story of the curing of the blind man will repay time and effort during Lent. And our prayer is that our eyes will be opened, so that we can begin to see things in a new way. In the Genesis story on the fall of our first parents we are told that 'their eyes were opened and they realised that they were naked'. Can we begin to see that without Christ our lives too are bereft, that we are naked?

8

The Raising of Lazarus (Jn, Ch. 11)

One of the most vibrant passages in the whole of the Old Testament must be the one from the Prophet Ezekiel:

> I am now going to open your graves; I mean to raise you from your graves, my people, and lead you back to the soil of Israel. And you will know that I am the Lord, when I open your graves and raise you from your graves, my people. And I shall put my spirit in you, and you will live...

Here too we are presented with the central theme of the Lenten readings, the notion of life, and Jesus as the life-giver. He has come to fulfil this promise of the prophet, to raise us up and give us new life. On the Sunday that has this reading from Ezekiel as the first reading, the gospel is the powerful story of the raising of Lazarus from the dead. The promise that is contained in this story is so incredible, so mind-blowing, as to be very difficult to believe. But our problem is that we have heard it so often that the power, the awesomeness, of the story is almost completely lost on us.

Lazarus and his sisters, Mary and Martha, were friends of Jesus, and when he got seriously ill they managed to get a message to him.

> *The man you love is ill.*

For some reason Jesus did not hurry down to them. He had been in Judea recently, and the authorities were threatening his life, so the disciples felt it would not be wise of him to go down again so soon. He waited a few days, and then he set off.

Martha met him at the outskirts of the village:

> *Lord, if you had been here my brother would not have died.*

A simple statement of fact as she saw it, and possibly with a slight element of reproach to it, that was repeated a little later by Mary when she too came out and saw him. They had total confidence that he would not have allowed this to happen if he had been present. Even still, Martha was clearly not without hope.

> *But even now I know that whatever you ask of God he will grant it to you.*

When Jesus said that her brother would rise again, she took it to mean that he was talking about the resurrection on the last day. But then he came out with one of these enormous statements that he tended to make every now and again. It is used so often now, particularly at funeral Masses, that it has lost its power for us, which is a pity.

I am the resurrection.
If anyone believes in me, even though he dies he will live,
And whoever lives and believes in me will never die.

When he asked Martha if she believed what he had just said we have no way of knowing at what level she was hearing it. But she comes back with her statement of faith.

I believe that you are the Christ, the Son of God, the one who was to come into the world.

Martha was the practical one, but it seems as if Jesus had a closer emotional connection with Mary, because when she came out to him he began to cry, and 'with a sigh that came straight from the heart', asked where the body was. The people standing around must have become extraordinarily interested at this point. They had heard so much about this man, so many stories of wonder working. What was going to happen? The way the story is told from here on is terse, almost cryptic. A minimum of words is used, and there is endless scope for the imagination. When they reached the tomb he simply asked that the big stone covering the entrance be rolled away.

Take the stone away.

If he wanted to heighten the tension and anticipation around him this was the perfect way to do it. The crowd must have been on their toes, straining to see into the dark hole where the body lay. The cloth Lazarus was wrapped in was probably white, so the chances are they could see some outline of the body in the semi-darkness. What was going to happen? This was surely a significant moment in the life of Jesus. The man who talked so much about life, who promised that those who believed in him would have the fullness of life, and eternal life, was now face to face with death. He had raised people from the dead before, but the fact that Lazarus was four days in the tomb somehow sets this one apart. It was almost as if he had given himself this final test, and doing it publicly so that the result would be plain to be seen by everyone. Life stood at that tomb, in direct opposition to death, and they all waited to see what would happen.

Once more it is the simplicity of what Jesus said that is striking:

Lazarus, come out!

Somewhere in the recesses of Lazarus' deadness he heard that call. The story only tells us that he came out, with his hands and his feet all bound. I wonder how he got out. He couldn't have stood up and walked if he was bound. He must have crawled out, or rolled out. But he got out. We all would, if we were lying in a black hole, lost in our deadness and we heard the voice calling us to life. Maybe at this moment he was lying in a heap on the ground at Jesus' feet, but with his eyes open blinking against the bright light. We might have expected Jesus to say something to him, maybe to welcome him back from the dead. Instead he turned and spoke to the people, and his words again spell out his mission in the world.

Unbind him and let him go free.

For the Jews the notion of freedom from captivity was a big thing, dating back to the story of Moses rescuing them from slavery in Egypt. To set a person free would have strong resonance for them. And this is how Jesus had come to see his mission. He was here to unbind us, to set us free from all that is shackling us, holding us back from being the fully alive people he wants us to be.

I have come that you may have life, life in all its fullness.

The implication is that Lazarus did not just rise to his old life, but that he rose to a fuller, deeper, more worthwhile life than he had in the past, the life lived by a person who has come to know the Kingdom of God.

Of course, like all the stories in John's Gospel, there are many levels at which we can understand this one. We don't have to be in the tomb to be dead. We can be dead in many ways, by not living our lives to the full. During Lent we try to work out what are the things that are binding us, deadening us.

We can be bound by fear. Maybe it is even something we brought from our childhood that makes us cautious, afraid, unable to take the chances necessary for full living, always waiting for someone to catch us out.

We can be shackled by scruples, weighed down with anxiety because we view God as a hard taskmaster who will be waiting for us when we die with a ledger, to make us account for every little detail of our lives.

Some event in our past may have hurt us so deeply that we haven't got over it, and it spoils our lives. We are not able to forgive someone for something they did to us, or maybe we don't want to forgive; we are afraid that we will lose some integral part of ourselves if we let go of our hurt.

We may be addicted to something in a way that makes us a slave to that addiction.

We may be full of disappointment that our lives have not turned out as we had hoped. Opportunities did not come our way, or if they did we may have missed them, and we feel cheated by life. We are so busy regretting what might have been, that we fail to live what we have.

We may have settled for less in life, because the effort necessary to bring out our full potential is too much for us. It's easier to take the soft option.

An important relationship, one that gave great promise, has turned out to be less than we had hoped, or has broken up, and we have become embittered. In our disillusionment we cannot summon up the energy to do something about it, or to try again.

There are a thousand ways in which we can be dead, in which the energy and vitality can be gone from various areas of our life. Jesus is calling us too, just as he called Lazarus, to come out of that tomb. He is telling us come out, to let him unbind us from what is shackling us, and let us go free.

The raising of Lazarus is not just a message about eternal life. It is also a message for this life too, and it is the message of Lent and indeed of the whole of Christianity. Jesus has come to give us life, and we are free to choose how we live our lives.

9

Jesus on the Side of the Oppressed

Christianity has had a chequered history. On the one hand the message has been kept alive in some form or other and passed on to our time, and that is a major achievement in itself. Maybe some of the purity of the message has sometimes been lost along the way. There were periods in history when it went badly eschew, leading to wars and persecutions. But in spite of all this the faith has come to us sufficiently alive to interest people, to excite them, and even to get some to dedicate their lives in one form or another to the person who first presented the message, Jesus Christ. That is all good. But the biggest fault of Christian churches down through the centuries in my view was the frequency with which they allied themselves with the people in power, and even at times became part of the power structure itself. Precisely the temptation that faced Jesus when the devil showed him all the kingdoms of the world, and promised to give them to him, is the temptation that all to often the Church has succumbed to.

One of the very impressive things about Jesus was the consistency with which he stood for the powerless, the oppressed, the poor. Some of the Lenten Gospel stories illustrate that clearly.

The Temple was a very large compound in the time of Jesus. It needed to be, since it was part of the duty of every Jew to visit there each year, to pray and to offer sacrifice. The various parts of the Temple led inwards, to the Holy of Holies, the resting place of the Ark of the Covenant, which could only be entered by the Chief Priest. Priests in that society were very different to our notion of priest. The nearest equivalent to our priest was the pharisee, who was the leader of the local synagogue. The sole function of the Jewish priest was to work within the Temple. They ran the system there, and tended to the needs of the constant flow of pilgrims. But they were very influential. Jesus came into conflict with them many times and it was the chief priest, Annas, and his father-in-law Caiaphas, who were mostly instrumental in having him put to death. In those days Judea was part of the Roman Empire, and the currency of the empire, with the head of Caesar on it, was used in ordinary commerce. But the priests would not allow this currency into the Temple, for the stated reason that it would be sacrilege, since the Emperor of Rome claimed divine power. Instead they had their own currency for use only in the Temple. Each person who visited the Temple had to offer in sacrifice a bird or an animal, and the priests decreed that these could not be brought in, but had to be purchased within the Temple compound. It was undoubtedly a cosy cartel, to use a modern phrase. So everybody had to change money as they came into the Temple. This is why the money changers were so busy. The story tells us that Jesus made a whip and drove them all out of the Temple, scattering the coins and knocking over the tables. The traditional interpretation of that story was that Jesus considered that the commercial transactions were desecrating the sacred precincts.

Stop turning my father's house into a market-place.

There will inevitably be tension between the Christian and the world of commerce, the material world, because one is based on the promotion of self-interest, and the other on love of the neighbour. But another interpretation of the story, and for me a more demanding one, is that Jesus was angered by the fact that the Temple authorities charged such exorbitant rates of exchange, and that they were exploiting the poor people who came to pray. It is the view of most scholars that Jesus' actions on this day precipitated the final conflict between himself and the priests.

The woman caught in adultery is one of the most commonly used stories from the Gospels. It is rich in drama, and beautifully told, like all the stories in John's Gospel, painting the picture in stark, clear terms. It is another good illustration of Jesus standing up for the underdog. It is hard for us today to realise the lowly status women occupied in that society. It has often been remarked that the woman's accomplice in the act of adultery was nowhere to be seen, even though they had been caught together in the act. But that would have been totally accepted at the time. The woman was to blame, and must take the consequences. And the consequences were terrible, death by stoning. A similar attitude still prevails in some Muslim countries, and remnants of this line of thought can also sometimes be found among ourselves. But once again Jesus, who in himself was the perfect example of the Kingdom of God, looked at the situation and the woman very differently from all the others. He had eyes that could see, and he saw through to the human being in front of him, and what she needed. The scribes and the Pharisees, who had brought the woman to him, were blinded by their legalism. Having dismissed the accusers with great skill, using a biblical version of the adage that people in glass houses shouldn't throw stones, Jesus turned to the woman and told her to go in peace and not to sin again. What exactly did Jesus mean by this last sentence? Was it a threat? Don't sin again or you will be condemned in the next life and sent to Hell. I don't think so. Taken in the context of Jesus' teaching on the Kingdom it is clearly an exhortation to turn away from a destructive style of life, and instead to begin to live her life more fully. In other words Jesus, as was his wont, was calling on this woman to open her eyes, to see the destructiveness of her way of living, and with new eyes seeing a new way, to begin to live anew.

The other Lenten Gospel where we see Jesus looking at things in a new way is the one where he calls on people not to make a show of their virtue. When you give alms, do not let your left hand know what your right hand is doing. When you pray do so quietly, and don't make a show of it. And when you fast don't look gloomy in order to show everyone what you are doing. In other words, don't puff yourself up and try to make a great person out of yourself. Do it all quietly.

The picture of the follower of Christ that is painted here is of someone who is remarkably free of self importance, and of all types of greed, but whose focus is other people and what is best for them. He or she is willing to put him or herself on the line in order to stand with the most downtrodden and oppressed. Here the Lenten message takes on a sharp edge, and begins to make major demands on all of us. It is good to believe in Jesus, to practice our religion, and to pray, but we must go much farther than that. We must let our beliefs be seen in the way we live.

The Gospel of the second Sunday of Lent is the story of the Transfiguration, that mysterious tale of Jesus on the top of the mountain with Peter, James and John. His form changes, taking on a heavenly appearance, and he is talking to some of the ancient prophets. Peter is so taken by this experience that he wants to stay there. 'Let us build three tents…'. But the scene fades, and they have to return down the mountain, and take up their lives.

It is the same with us. Religious experiences are good, indeed important, but the real test is to be found in trying to follow his example in our daily lives:

This is my Son, the Beloved. Listen to him.

10

Harden not your Hearts

Harden not your hearts today, but listen to the voice of the Lord.

Jesus identified hardness of heart as the big obstacle to building the Kingdom of God. By a hard heart he meant a heart that is set on its own way of thinking and living, and is not open to new ways of thinking, new ways of looking at things. An essential element of the Kingdom of God is precisely this opening of our eyes, this new way of seeing. As long as a person's heart remains hard change will be very difficult. The essential requirement for change is a fresh outlook, a new understanding. From this new understanding a new lifestyle can begin. Hardness of heart is common. Most of us suffer from it at some time or other in our lives.

But God has his way of helping us to deal with it.

I will take away your heart of stone
And give you a heart of flesh instead.

This Scripture text has sometimes been interpreted too narrowly. We saw it as referring to a person who is living a deeply sinful life, and will not give up their sinfulness. But where Jesus found the most incorrigible hardness of heart was among those who would have regarded themselves as the good-living people in the society, particularly the religious leaders. It is a frightening thought that when we think we are living good lives we can have the greatest difficulty with hardness of heart. We believe we are right, and that we don't need to change. And this often goes hand in hand with a facility at recognising the faults of others, and passing judgement on them.

> *Those who believe with complete certainty that they are right are dark inside, and darken the world around them with cruelty, pain and injustice.*

Hardness of heart also comes when we allow ourselves to be locked into the events or experiences of our past. That attitude is prevalent today, and is often encouraged by public opinion. People say things like 'My life was destroyed when he did that to me'. While we can feel sympathy for people in this situation, it too is hardness of heart. The hard heart is the heart that is not capable of change, of letting go, of forgiving, no matter what the reason.

So, when we pray in the words of the Psalm, '*A pure heart create for me, O God*', we are praying for a heart that is open, open to the vision and the values of the Kingdom, and willing to change. It is also a heart that is full of compassion for the struggling fellow human being. This sort of compassion is more often found among the strugglers themselves, people who have failed so often in their own lives that they understand the weakness of others. It is very much a 'Kingdom of God' way of looking at things.

An important theme of the Lenten readings, just as it is also during Advent, is that there is always hope, hope for everyone.

We can be so sure of this because there is no limit or depth to the compassion of Jesus.

> I pray that ... you, together with all God's people, may have the power to understand the breadth, the length, the height and the depth of Christ's love. (St Paul)

This is very obvious in the Lenten Gospel stories. No matter what a mess our lives are in, no matter how deeply buried we are in failure or sin, no matter how close to despair, Jesus has the message of hope. And he does not reject anyone, not the rich man whom he asked to sell all that he had so he could be free, nor the woman at the well in Samaria who had the five husbands, nor the blind man, or the woman caught in adultery. St Paul puts it plainly:

> With God on our side, who can be against us?...
> Who can separate us from the love of Christ?
> Can trouble do it, or hardship, or persecution, or hunger, or poverty, or danger, or death?
> No! In all these things we have complete victory through Him who loved us.
> For I am certain that nothing can separate us from his love.
> Neither death nor life, neither angels nor other heavenly rulers or powers, neither the present nor the future, neither the world above nor the world below;
> There is nothing in all creation that will ever be able to separate us from the love of God which is ours through Christ Jesus our Lord.

Or elsewhere Paul writes:

> *God loved the world with so much love that he was generous with his mercy.*

Jesus expressed this himself in an even more emphatic manner, when he was speaking to Nicodemus:

> *Yes, God loved the world so much that he gave his only Son,*
> *so that everyone who believes in him may not be lost*
> *but may have eternal life.*
> *For God sent his Son into the world not to condemn the world,*
> *but so that through him the world might be saved.*

Too often, we in the Christian churches have preached condemnation, and the exclusive nature of salvation, that it would only be available to a few. It suited us to believe that we would have Heaven to ourselves. The American writer, Flannery O'Connor, in one of her short stories gives a description of the shock on the faces of the 'good people' as they bring up the rear of the procession into Heaven, with all the people they had looked down on all their lives leading the way. Jesus did not come to condemn, but to save.

Isaiah was the great prophet of the life and mission of Jesus. This is how he expresses it.

> *No need to recall the past,*
> *no need to think about what has gone before.*
> *See, I am doing a new deed,*
> *even now it comes to light; can you not see it?*
> *Yes, I am making a road in the wilderness,*
> *paths in the wilds.*

The wild beasts will honour me,
jackals and ostriches,
because I am putting water in the wilderness,
rivers in the wild
to give my chosen people drink.

Yes, surely a new creation, a creation built out of the love of God for his people. It is a creation where the past does not rule us, where we can change, where we can find a safe path in the wilderness of our loneliness and fear, where our weariness will be washed away, and where we will have new energy. This is the Lenten message, just as it is the message of the whole of Christianity. The Kingdom of God is at hand. It is a Kingdom built on love, and enduring through love. This is both our hope and our challenge.

11

The Passion Story

The Passion story, the story of the suffering and death of Jesus, is central to the faith of a Christian. It has enormous resonance for all of us brought up in the faith. We can remember trying to stand still while it was read at the Palm Sunday Mass or on Good Friday, in the hope that if we succeeded in not moving we would gain a plenary indulgence. Each of the four Gospels tells the story, with no major variations between them. It is the story of the apparent victory of hate over love, of conspiracy over honesty, of sin over goodness, and ultimately of evil over good. It is a terrible story, where an obviously good and innocent man is brutally tortured and put to a shameful and horrific death. But like so much of the life and teaching of Jesus, the Passion story has lost a lot of its power over us, because we have heard it so often, and now it is difficult for us to hear it with new ears.

In recent years I have attempted to present the Passion in new and fresh ways, while at the same time remaining as faithful to the text as possible. The following is one of these attempts.

The narrator of the story could be any of the apostles, except Peter, who as an old man hears part of the Scripture account being read, and the memories of those terrible days come flooding back to him. He begins to tell his story. I intersperse his account with passages from the text. For effective public presentation it is also good to have some music and singing, for example verses of 'Were you there when they crucified my Lord?', or the Reproaches, with the people singing the response, 'O my people, what have I done to you, how have I hurt you? Answer me'.

The Passion Story

Judas Iscariot, one of the twelve, approached the chief priests with an offer to hand Jesus over to them. They were delighted to hear it, and promised to give him money; and he looked for a way of betraying him when the opportunity should occur.

We knew that Judas could not be trusted. He was always a slippery character. But Jesus could be naïve at times; at least we thought so. He was inclined to trust people even if all the evidence suggested that he shouldn't. When he put Judas in charge of the money we knew there would be trouble; we warned him, but he didn't change his mind.

But first there was the Passover Meal, the biggest night of the year for us Jews. Two people had gone ahead to get everything ready, and when evening came we all assembled. Unfortunately, what I remember from that night was not the celebration; it was the sense of foreboding, the heaviness in the air, the feeling that something terrible was going to happen.

And as they were eating he took some bread, and when he had said the blessing he broke it and gave it to them, saying: Take it, this is my body.

Then he took the cup, and when he had returned thanks he gave it to them, and all drank from it, and he said to them: This is my blood, the blood of the covenant, which is to be poured out for many.

That meal was different to any other meal we had with him; we sensed that it would be our last, that he was leaving us.

And when he took the bread and the cup, and gave them to us — of course we didn't understand the full meaning of what was happening.

But we would have taken anything from him that night, we loved him so much, and we did not want to lose him. We wanted him to remain with us forever. How could we live without him?

Then the meal was over. There was a garden close by where we had gone before; it was a quiet spot. We went there that night.

Again he went away and prayed, saying the same words. And once more he came back and found them sleeping, their eyes were so heavy; and they could find no answer for him

He came back a third time and said to them: You can sleep on now and take your rest. It is all over. The hour has come. My betrayer is close at hand.

When we got to the garden he went away on his own. The account says that we slept. If I did, it was more like a nightmare. I could hear his voice crying in the distance: 'Let this chalice pass from me'.

Then he came over to us, and what he said was not an accusation, it was more an appeal: 'Could you not watch one hour with me?' He seemed so vulnerable, so afraid. We had never seen him like this before.

The soldiers came with Judas. He did a terrible thing; it really showed up the type of man he was; he identified Jesus with a kiss, using the gesture of affection as his act of betrayal. We weren't surprised.

But neither did we cover ourselves with glory that night. I am ashamed to think of it...

And they all deserted him, and ran away...

That is what we did; we ran away!

The soldiers brought him before the High Priest. We knew there was no possibility of justice there. The priests hated Jesus; he had criticised them too often, and they weren't good at taking criticism. He hadn't a hope in their court.

And they all gave their verdict: he deserved to die. Some of them started spitting at him and blindfolding him, they began hitting him with their fists and shouting.

I gradually picked up my courage and made my way to the palace of the High Priest. It was a cold night, and I joined a crowd standing around a fire. I was relieved to see that Peter was there too. After Jesus he was the one we looked up to; maybe he would know how to rescue Jesus.

But then I couldn't believe what I heard happening. A little slip of a servant girl looked up at Peter, and said: 'Aren't you one of this man's followers?' I expected Peter to use this as a spur to action. But instead he answered; 'I do not know him'. I looked over at Peter, but he would not meet my eyes.

At that moment the cock crew for the second time, and Peter recalled how Jesus had said to him: Before the cock crows twice you will have disowned me three times, and he burst into tears.

The priests had no doubt about their judgement, but they hadn't the power to execute him, so they sent him off to Pilate. Pilate wasn't a bad man; he just didn't care. He didn't understand our people. All he wanted to do was to get back to Rome, away from this uncomfortable outpost with its interminable religious quarrels. And he didn't want any bad reports going back that might interfere with his promotion. He had nothing at all against Jesus, but when the pressure came on he gave in easily.

Pilate said: What am I to do with the man you call King of the Jews?
They shouted back: Crucify him.
Why? What harm has he done?
But they shouted all the more loudly: Crucify him.

They got their wish. Pilate agreed that he would be crucified.

They laid the large crossbeam on his shoulders, and he set out on the journey to the top of the Hill of Calvary. I followed at a distance.

What I remember mostly of that interminable journey was the venom of the crowd, how much they hated him; some of them were the same people who had welcomed him into the city just a few days previously; the abuse they shouted, the spitting, the cursing.

And then when we got to the top of the hill, the sound of the nails being driven into his hands; those hands that had been used so much to bless and to comfort, to heal all types of illness.

Finally I saw the big cross rise against the sky, with him hanging on it. I couldn't bear to look.

They offered him wine mixed with myrrh, but he refused it. Then they crucified him, and shared out his clothing, casting lots to decide what each should get.

It was the third hour when they crucified him.

What I remember of the next three hours is the darkness. They say that the sun stopped shining. That may well have happened. All I know is that for me everything was dark for those three hours; the darkness of despair was in my heart.

Here was the man I had left everything to follow, the man on whom I had based all my hopes. He had said and done such wonderful things, and had given us all a vision of a new way of life. We had even come to believe that he was the Messiah, the one who had been promised. And there he was, hanging like a criminal on a cross. Was that how it was to end?

All my hope was gone.

At the ninth hour Jesus cried out in a loud voice:
My God, my God, why have you deserted me?

You cannot imagine how that cry made my blood run cold. We believed that he was the Son of God, the one who had come to save us. If God deserted him, what chance was there for the rest of us? Now indeed it was dark.

Jesus gave a loud cry, and he breathed his last.

When we saw that he was dead a few of us moved closer, and joined the women at the foot of the Cross. The women had never left him; they hadn't run away, like us. They had been faithful to the end. We took the body down, and after a hasty preparation, we placed him in a tomb given to us by Nicodemus.

The sun was just going down, and the Sabbath was beginning. We went home.

12

He is not here; He is risen

The great thing about Lent and Holy Week is that the story has a happy ending, the ultimate happy ending. Christ did not remain in that tomb, but rose from the dead, and is alive and with us.

The Easter Vigil ceremony is not one of the better attended of church services; it has got itself a bad name through being too long, with two many difficult and interminable readings. But there are lovely parts to this ceremony, especially the celebration of light.

The part that speaks most to me is the Easter Proclamation, or, as we used know it, the Exultet. A few of the verses might be worth spending a little time on as you prepare for the ceremony.

> *Rejoice, O earth, in shining splendour,*
> *radiant in the brightness of your King!*
> *Christ has conquered! Glory fills you!*
> *Darkness vanishes for ever!*

The promise that there will be no more darkness is wonderful; it is another way of saying that our hope is secure, that we will not be left helpless, that he will never fail us.

This is the night when Jesus Christ
broke the chains of death
and rose triumphant from the grave.
What good would life have been to us,
had Christ not come as our Redeemer?

It is hard for us, brought up as Christians, and coming from a long tradition of Christianity, to appreciate what a gift our faith is to us. On this night it is good to try to stand back for a moment and wonder what life would be like without Christ.

The power of this holy night
dispels all evil, washes guilt away,
restores lost innocence, brings mourners joy;
it casts out hatred, brings us peace, and humbles earthly pride.

Because of this night there is a new creation. The world will never be the same again. Wonderful things have happened for us and for all creation.

And then it is all summed up in that sentence from Luke's Gospel.

Why look among the dead for someone who is alive? He is not here! He
is risen!

Of course he is risen. He came to give us life, so it was not possible that he would be conquered by death. The light of the world could not be put out. The Kingdom of God is at hand.

It is Easter time. Let us celebrate!